Table of Contents

INTRODUCTION

Apple as a company has always found a way to improve on the consumers' endless need for more in a smartphone. From the first generation iPhone to the latest iPhone SE 2020, iPhones have proven to be a "game-changer" for the mobile phone industry as it is one of the most widely purchased and used smartphones currently in the world. More than 2.2 billion iPhones as of November 1, 2018, have been sold and more are still selling to date. This high acceptance and patronage from smartphone users all over the world are attributed to the uniqueness, simplicity, durability, and availability of iPhones. So far, among the thirteen generations of iPhones, Apple has been able to utilize its unique operating system

(OS) popularly called iOS (renamed iOS in 2010) which updates over the air, to allow iPhones operate seamlessly, multitask as well as possess good graphics compared to most of its counterparts in the phone market. The availability of various numerous applications (over 2.2million apps.) on iPhones via its App store makes its user experience worthwhile.

Apple driven with the sole purpose of maximum satisfaction and a bid to get more users to purchase and use their devices had to introduce a phone with so much more at a budget price. This is evident in the slogan for the promotion of this budget phone *"Lots of love. Less to spend"*. Yes!! I'm talking about the iPhone SE 2020 also known as the iPhone SE2.

This smartphone announced on April 15, 2020, is a 13th generation iPhone designed to replace the iPhone 8 series and succeed its predecessor- the first generation iPhone SE.

The first generation iPhone SE also known as the iPhone SE 1 is the 9th generation iPhone. The idea behind this design was to produce an iPhone that was portable, efficient, and quite affordable. Hence, its promotion slogan *"A big step for small"*. With its 4-inch screen, it was easier for users to navigate through the multipurpose touch screen especially while holding with one hand. It has almost the same external design as its predecessor iPhone 5S but has higher internal hardware, battery capacity, and improved rear camera (12-megapixel) hence the acronym *"SE"* which stands for *Special Edition.* This iPhone was however discontinued on September 12, 2018, with reasons best known to Apple.

Apple launched the iPhone SE 2020 which has been positioned as a budget smartphone in the phone market to target the average income earners, users who fancy small-sized phones, and also to address the demands for a successor of the first-generation iPhone SE. This they did remarkably well, as this new iPhone is a hybrid of the iPhone 8 and the iPhone 11 series. It shares the physical dimensions, size, and the single-camera lens of the iPhone 8 while also sharing some internal hardware components of the iPhone 11 series. No wonder! It was also marketed with this slogan *"A powerful new smartphone in a popular design"*.

This book is geared towards providing insight and in-depth knowledge about this new iPhone as well as serve as a user guide thus making the new iPhone SE your best choice and best companion in the year 2020.

THE IPHONE SE 2020

DESIGN/AVAILABILITY

The iPhone SE 2020 features a 4.7-inch (diagonal) screen (which is about thirty percent larger than its first-generation model) with thick bezels at the top and bottom of the iPhone. The top bezel presents a cutout for the speaker, front camera, and sensors while the bottom bezel has a central Home button. The iPhone SE has an aluminum frame, a glass front, and back which houses a single-lens rear camera, a microphone, and an LED flash. On the right side of the device, features a power button, the left side features a mute switch and volume buttons while the bottom features speaker holes and Lightning cable port. The iPhone SE 2020 measures 67.3mm wide,

138.4mm tall, 7.33mm thick, and weighs 5.22 ounces thus sharing the same physical dimension as the iPhone 8. This means that phone cases designed for the iPhone 8 can easily fit the iPhone SE 2020.

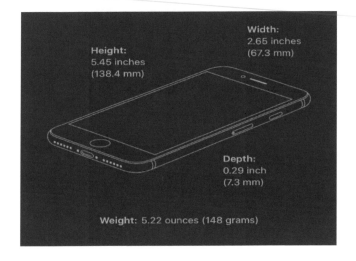

Photo credit: Apple

That's a good one from Apple! The iPhone SE is available in three colors: White, Black, and a (PRODUCT)Red edition. It's is available in 64GB, 128GB, and 256GB for users.

HARDWARE

THE A13 BIONIC SYSTEM ON CHIP

The iPhone SE features the Apple A13 Bionic system-on-chip. This is the fastest chip ever designed for a smartphone and as such provides unparalleled performance for every task. This means top-notch photography experience, improved augmented reality, and great gaming experience. The A13 Bionic chip also enables great battery life and power. The iPhone SE also incorporates a third-generation neural engine and an integrated M13 motion coprocessor. I think with all these, the iPhone SE is one of those extremely efficient smartphones available in the phone market.

CAMERA

The iPhone SE presents a single 12MP rear camera with an aperture of f/1.8, a quad-LED True Tone flash, and autofocus capable of recording 4K video (at 24, 30, or 60 fps), 1080p HD video (at 30, or 60 fps) or even 720p HD video (at 30 fps). It also presents a 7MP front camera with an aperture of f/2.2 and autofocus capable of shooting 1080p HD video at 30fps. With the use of the image signal processor and the Neural Engine of A13 Bionic combined, the iPhone SE becomes the best single-camera iPhone ever as it harnesses more benefits of computational photography. By employing machine learning and monocular depth estimation, both the front and rear cameras of the iPhone SE support Portrait mode and Portrait

Lighting effects taking stunning portraits and also Next-generation Smart HDR pictures with more natural details. Videos are now more fascinating with better cinematic stabilization and stereo audio recording on both front and rear cameras. The rear camera especially supports extended dynamic range videos up to 30fps and also high-quality video capture at 4K up to 60 fps. What's more interesting is that users can now record videos without switching out of photo mode by taking advantage of the *QuickTake video* on the front and rear cameras.

DISPLAY

The iPhone SE features a Retina HD display with wide color gamut which offers spectacular color accuracy as well as supports Dolby Vision and HDR playback and True Tone which adjusts the white balance to equal the ambient light for a better natural viewing experience. The LCD has a resolution of 1334×750 pixels and a pixel density of 326PPI. The iPhone SE uses Hepatic touch for Quick Actions such as previewing messages, animating Live photos, and rearranging apps.

TOUCH ID

The iPhone SE features a home button with a Touch ID fingerprint sensor covered with a steel ring that detects a user's fingerprint. The Touch ID is used to unlock the iPhone, confirm App Store purchases, confirm Apple Pay transactions, open passcode-protected apps, and fill in passwords with iCloud Keychain. The Touch ID sensor is protected by a durable sapphire crystal.

BATTERY

The iPhone SE uses a 1,821 mAh battery capacity that supports fast charging. This means it can be charged to 50% battery life in just 30 minutes and it is enabled using a USB-C power adapter an of at least 18 watts and a USB-C Lightning cable. The iPhone SE also supports wireless charging as it has a glass body with a built-in wireless charging coil that supports Qi-based wireless charging. The battery lasts for up to 8 hours of streaming video playback, 13 hours of video playback, and up to 40 hours of audio playback.

DUAL-SIM FEATURE

The iPhone SE supports the Dual-Sim functionality as it allows the use of two phone numbers at a time through the use of a physical Nano-SIM and an eSIM.

Wi-Fi AND BLUETOOTH

The iPhone SE supports Wi-Fi 6 with 2×2 MIMO which is the latest Wi-Fi protocol and allows download up to 38% faster than other Wi-Fi protocols like the Wi-Fi 5. That's a nice one from Apple!

It also supports Bluetooth 5.0 which offers faster speed, larger broadcast message capacity, and longer range.

SOFTWARE

The iPhone SE was officially shipped with iOS 13.4 that supports Apple Pay and Apple Card after which a software update (iOS 13.4.1) was available on the day before the release date of the device. However, on June 1st, Apple released a new update the iOS 13.5.1 and is available for download for the iPhone SE.

OTHER FEATURES

The iPhone SE features an IP67 rating (dust and water resistance of water at a maximum depth of 1 meter for up to 30 minutes) under the International Electrotechnical Commission (IEC) standard. This device also features various sensors like the Barometer, Three-axis gyro, Accelerometer, Proximity sensor, and ambient light sensor. Accessibility features are not left out as Apple has once again provided built-in support for hearing, vision, and mobility via some features like Speak Screen, Assistive Touch, Siri and Dictation, Zoom, VoiceOver and many more geared towards helping people with disabilities. For location services, the iPhone also features built-in GPS/GNSS, Digital compass, and iBeacon micro-location.

HOW TO SET UP YOUR IPHONE SE 2020

Now that you have gotten this your new smartphone, setting it up might just be an issue especially if new to the iPhone universe. As a user, you have to know your options when setting up. These options include;

- Setting up as a new iPhone - This is for people who've never used an iPhone or any Apple online service.

- Restoring from a previous iPhone - This is for people who've had a previous iOS device and are moving to a new one and want everything they had on the older device intact on the new device.

- Importing data from a non-iOS phone - This is for people

switching from a different mobile platform to an iPhone.

Having understood your options, you are just one step closer to setting up your new device. Please Note! Before the setting up process begins, you should take note of the following;

- There must be an available Cellular network. For instance, the device must be in a Verizon Wireless 3G or LTE area.
- If setting up in the absence of a Cellular network, an active Wi-Fi network must be available.
- Ensure the device is charged. If the battery is drained, use an AC adapter to charge for approximately 15 minutes.

SETTING UP AS A NEW IPHONE

- Turn on your new device - Press and hold the side button or power button until the Apple logo appears.
- Immediately, you would see "Hello" in different languages. Press Home to open and continue the setup.
- Select your preferred language.
- Select your country or region - This affects how information looks on your device, including time, date, and more.
- Tap Set Up manually.
- Select a Wi-Fi network or a Cellular Network depending on which is available.
- Apple's Data & Privacy information would be displayed next, Tap Continue after reading.

- Set Up Touch ID - Tap "Set Up Touch ID Later" or Tap Continue and follow the instructions as you would be prompted to place your thumb or finger on the Home button repeatedly. If prompted to change your grip, tap Continue and place your thumb or finger on the Home button repeatedly as directed then tap Continue.

- Create a Passcode - Enter a six-digit passcode or if you'd like a four-digit passcode or custom passcode, tap "Passcode Options." This allows the use of some features like Touch ID, Apple pay, some App purchases, and so on.

- Re-enter the passcode supplied and Tap Next.

- App & Data - Set up options would be displayed on the screen on how to transfer apps and data to this new device.
- Click on "Don't Transfer Apps & Data" to set up as a new device.
- Enter Apple ID and Password. If you don't have one, you can create a new one. Just Tap *Don't have an Apple ID?* and follow promptly. Tap Next.
- Read and Tap Agree to Apple's Terms and Conditions.
- Select Enable Location Services.
- Apple Pay – Tap Continue to Set up Apple Pay or click Set Up Later in Wallet.
- Tap Continue to Set up iCloud Keychain or Tap Set it Up Later in Settings.

- Tap Continue to Set up Siri and "Hey, Siri" or Tap Set it Up Later in Settings.
- Tap Continue to Set up Screen Time or Tap Set it Up in Settings.
- From the App Analytics screen, Click Share with App Developers or Don't Share (clicking "Don't share" saves battery life).
- Appearance – Select between Light or Dark mode display for your iPhone. Tap continue after selection.
- Display Zoom – Select how you want your display view; Standard or Zoomed out. Tap continue after selection.
- You would see "Welcome to iPhone".
- Click on "Get Started" to begin using your new device.

RESTORING FROM A PREVIOUS IPHONE

This is another way of setting up your new device. This procedure (Quick Start) is possible if your old iPhone and new iPhone are operating on iOS 11, 12.4, 13, or later (Note the iPhone SE 2020 is shipped with iOS 13.4 so it is compatible with this process). It allows you to transfer information quickly from your old device to the new device wirelessly. Either phone needs to have a charge or plugged into power because the process occupies both phones and any form of power interruption could affect the data transfer. It is also important to have a backup for your data (iCloud or iTunes) especially if you are running on older iOS (11, 12.4) on your old device before embarking on this quick start process to ensure full transfer of data to your new device. If your old device is running on iOS 13 and later, there is no need for a backup except you just want to.

HOW TO USE QUICK START

- Turn on your new device - Press and hold the side button or power button until the Apple logo appears.
- Immediately, you would see "Hello" in different languages. Press Home to open and continue to choose your preferred language.
- Place your new device near your old device that's using iOS 11 or later. Immediately, the QuickStart screen appears on your old device and offers

the option of using your Apple ID to set up your new device.

- Ensure that's the Apple ID you want to use, and then tap Continue. If you don't see the option to continue on your old device, make sure that Bluetooth is turned on.
- Immediately an animation will appear on your new device.
- Hold your old device over the new device, then center the animation in the viewfinder of your old device.
- Immediately a message that says "Finish on New [Device]" would appear. If you can't use your old device's camera, Click Authenticate Manually, then keenly follow the steps that appear.

- Enter your old device's passcode on your new device.
- Follow the instructions to set up Touch ID on your new device or choose to Set Up Later.
- Transfer Your Data – This gives you two options; transfer data from iPhone (old) or download data from iCloud. My advice is that you, Tap on Transfer data from iPhone especially if your old device is operating on iOS 13 and later because it is faster except you prefer downloading from iCloud if you already have an existing backup.
- Read and Tap Agree to Apple's Terms and Conditions.

- Select Customize or Continue to keep settings from your old iPhone.
- Select Enable Location Services.
- Apple Pay – Tap Continue to Set up Apple Pay or click Set Up Later in Wallet.
- Tap Continue to Set up Siri and "Hey, Siri" or Tap Set it Up Later in Settings.
- From the App Analytics screen, Tap Share with App Developers or Don't Share (choosing "Don't share" saves up battery)
- Immediately, the transfer of the data screen comes up on both the old device and new device showing the transfer progress.
- Wait patiently for the entire process to complete until a

message saying "Transfer complete" pops up on the old iPhone.

- Wait for your new device to reboot and get started with Apps downloading in the background.
- Viola! It's like magic. All your data on your old device which includes Photos, Videos, Contacts, and App data are now on your new iPhone SE 2020 in just minutes.

IMPORTING DATA FROM A NON-iOS PHONE

Most times we have non-iOS smartphone users all over the world who want to share in the iPhone experience. This means they would have to get a new iPhone to say the iPhone SE 2020 and as such would want to transfer all their data and files from their older smartphone. Apple has an app in Google Playstore that makes this possible and very easy. The app is called *Move to iOS* and should already be downloaded on the Android phone you wish to transfer from.

HOW DOES THIS WORK?

This is made possible through a direct Wi-Fi connection between the Android device and the iOS device. This connection is only established via the Move to iOS app and also when the iPhone is running on iOS 9 and higher. This connection only transfers photos, contacts, calendars, and accounts. It does not transfer apps, music, or any of your passwords.

PROCEDURE FOR THE TRANSFER

- Turn on your new device - Press and hold the side button or power button until the Apple logo appears.
- Immediately, you would see "Hello" in different languages. Press Home to open and continue the setup.
- Select your preferred language.
- Select your country or region - This affects how information looks on your device, including time, date, and more.
- Tap Set Up manually.
- Select a Wi-Fi network or a Cellular Network depending on which is available.
- Apple's Data & Privacy information would be displayed next, Tap Continue after reading.

- Set Up Touch ID - Tap "Set Up Touch ID Later" or Tap Continue and follow the instructions as you would be prompted to place your thumb or finger on the Home button repeatedly. If prompted to change your grip, tap Continue and place your thumb or finger on the Home button repeatedly as directed then tap Continue.
- Create a Passcode - Enter a six-digit passcode or if you'd like a four-digit passcode or custom passcode, tap "Passcode Options." This allows the use of some features like Touch ID, Apple pay, some App purchases, and so on.
- Re-enter the passcode supplied and Tap Next.

- App & Data - Set up options would be displayed on the screen on how to transfer apps and data to this new device.
- Select "Move Data from Android".
- Launch the Move to iOS app on the Android device
- Tap Continue on both devices.
- Tap Agree and then tap Next on Android device.
- Enter the 12-digit code displayed on the iPhone in your Android device.
- Once the code has been entered, the Android device would automatically connect with your iPhone over Wi-Fi.
- Once connected, you would see a list of items you would want to transfer on the Android device. Tick on any or all and Continue.

- After the completion of the transfer process, Tap on Continue Setting Up iPhone.
- Enter Apple ID and Password. If you don't have one, you can create a new one. Just Tap *Don't have an Apple ID?* and follow promptly. Tap Next.
- Read and Tap Agree to Apple's Terms and Conditions.
- Select Enable Location Services.
- Apple Pay – Tap Continue to Set up Apple Pay or click Set Up Later in Wallet.
- Tap Continue to Setup iCloud Keychain or Tap Set it Up Later in Settings.
- Tap Continue to Set up Siri and "Hey, Siri" or Tap Set it Up Later in Settings.

- Tap Continue to Set up Screen Time or Tap Set it Up in Settings.
- From the App Analytics screen, Tap Share with App Developers or Don't Share (choosing not to share saves battery life)
- Appearance – Select between Light or Dark mode display for your iPhone. Tap continue after selection.
- Display Zoom – Select how you want your display view; Standard or Zoomed out. Tap continue after selection.
- You would see "Welcome to iPhone".
- Tap "Get Started" to begin using your new device.
- After this, you would be prompted to log in to the

accounts that were transferred from the Android device.

- Do this, and you are good to go!

HOW TO IMPORT SIM CONTACTS TO YOUR NEW IPHONE SE 2020

Having have set up your new device and ready to enjoy your seamless iPhone experience, now would be the perfect time for inserting your SIM Card into your device if you haven't done so already. Mounting of your SIM card to the point of importing already existing contacts to your new device is very easy! All you have to do is;

- Eject the SIM tray using a SIM tray Ejector

- Mount your SIM on the tray properly. Note that the SIM card must be a Nano-SIM.
- Insert the tray containing the SIM into the new device.
- Wait to see if your Service bar changes to the Carrier Network.
- Once the Cellular Network is available, head to Settings
- Tap Contacts.
- Tap Import SIM Contacts.
- If asked, choose the location you want to import your SIM Contacts.
- Wait patiently for the import to complete.
- Open Contacts and make sure that your contacts imported correctly.

www.ingramcontent.com/pod-product-compliance
Lightning Source LLC
LaVergne TN
LVHW072052060326
832903LV00054B/411